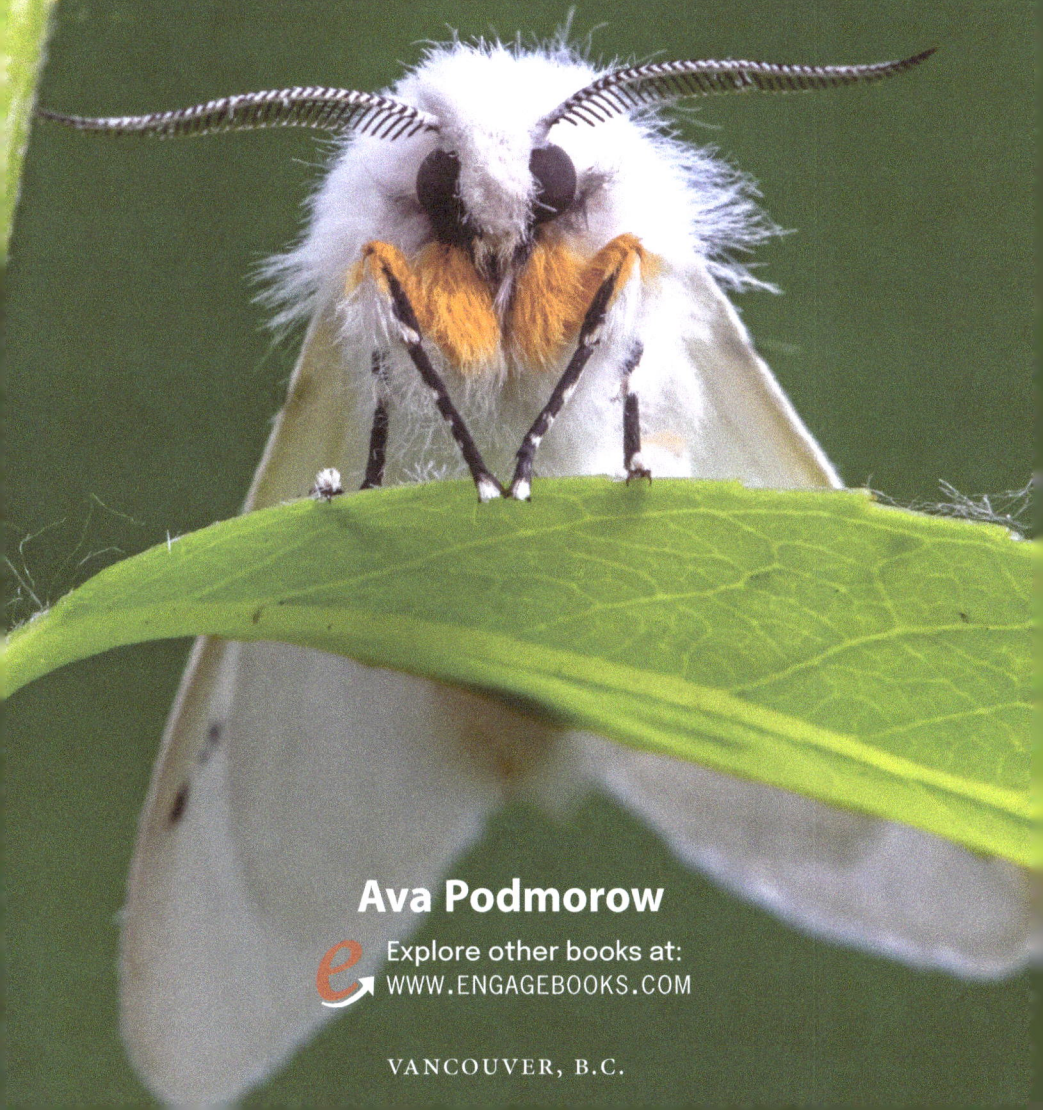

Backyard Bugs & Creepy-Crawlies

Moths

Ava Podmorow

Explore other books at:
WWW.ENGAGEBOOKS.COM

VANCOUVER, B.C.

WWW.ENGAGEBOOKS.COM

Moths: Level Pre-1
Backyard Bugs & Creepy Crawlies
Podmorow, Ava–2004
Text © 2022 Engage Books
Design © 2022 Engage Books

Edited by: A.R. Roumanis
and Sarah Harvey

Text set in Epilogue

FIRST EDITION / FIRST PRINTING

LIBRARY AND ARCHIVES CANADA CATALOGUING IN PUBLICATION

Title: Moths / Ava Podmorow.
Names: Podmorow, Ava, author.
Description: Series statement: Backyard bugs & creepy-crawlies
Engaging readers: level pre-1, beginner.

Identifiers: Canadiana (print) 20220403457 | Canadiana (ebook) 20220403465
ISBN 978-177476-712-2 (hardcover)
ISBN 978-177476-713-9 (softcover)
ISBN 978-177476-714-6 (epub)
ISBN 978-177476-715-3 (pdf)

Subjects:
LCSH: Moths—Juvenile literature.

Classification: LCC QL544.2 P63 2022 | DDC J595.78/9—DC23

This project has been made possible in part
by the Government of Canada.

Canada

Close the door!
Moths might get in!

3

Moths have two pairs of wings.

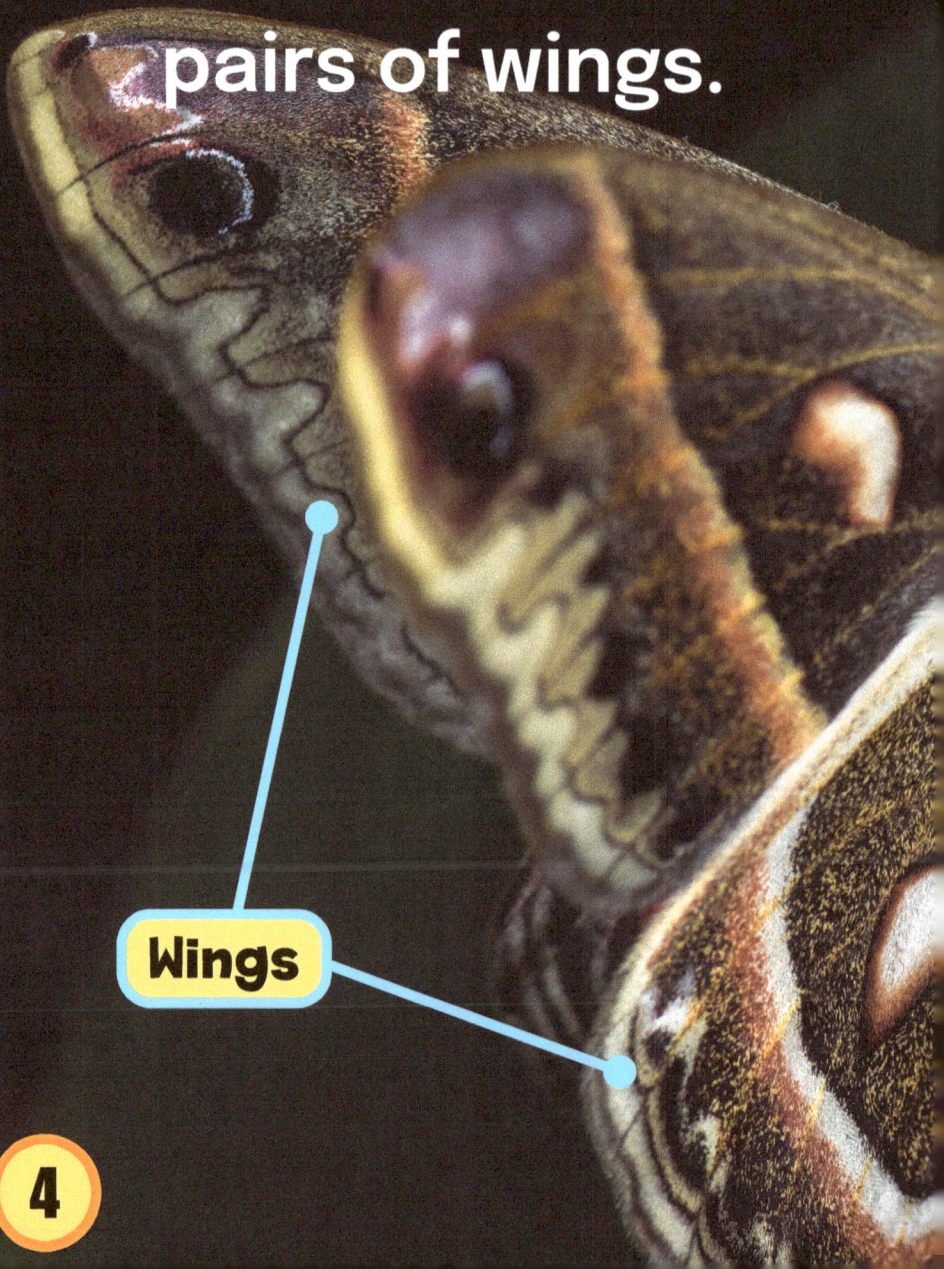

Wings

They have two antennae, and six legs.

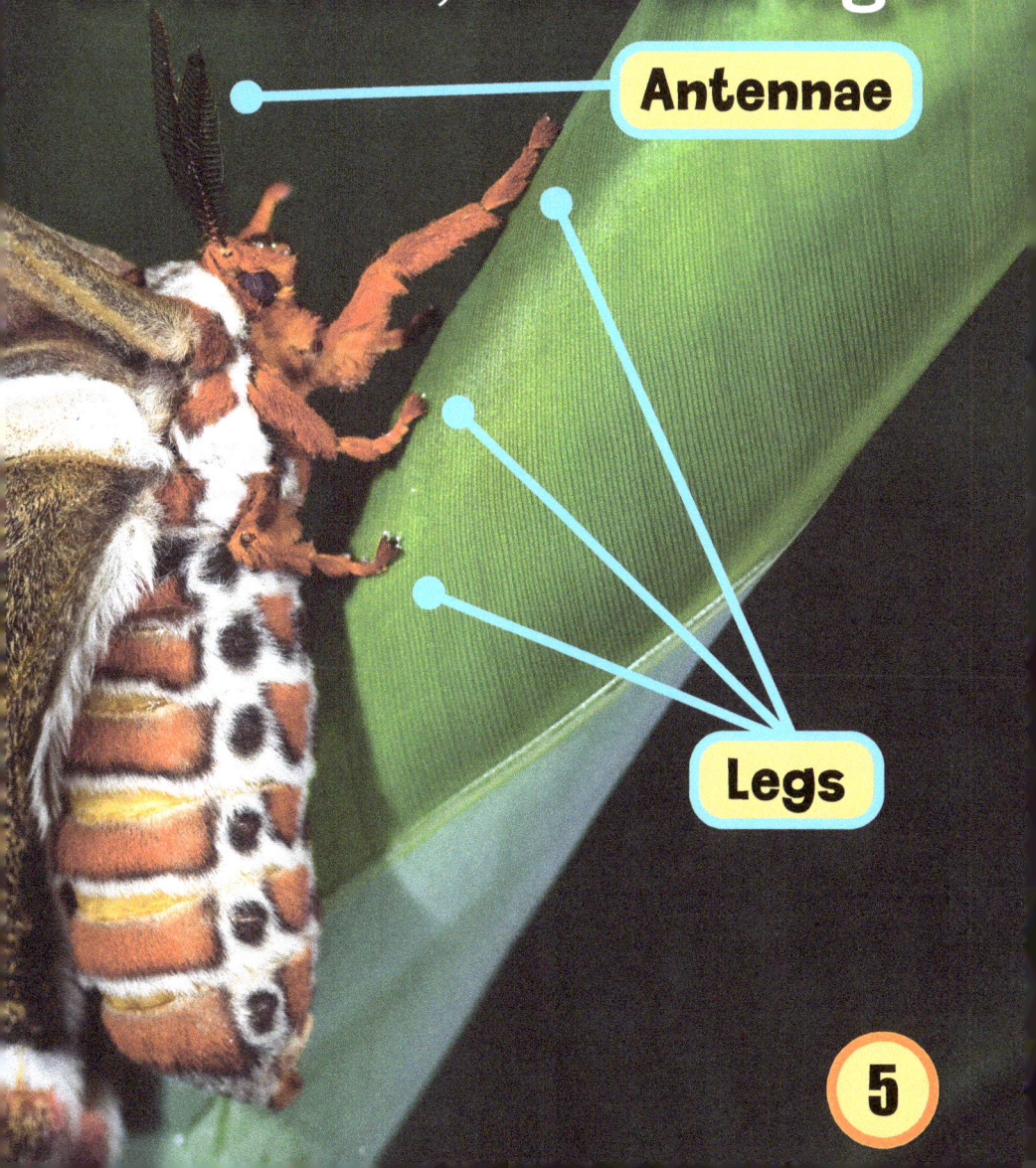

Antennae

Legs

Many moths eat fruits and vegetables.

Others chew on
dark wool clothing.

Most moths like to
be near light.

The moths that eat clothing like to be in the dark.

Luna moths
do not need
to eat at all.

They live on the food they stored when they were caterpillars.

There are over 150,000 kinds of moths.

The biggest moth is the Hercules moth.

Hercules moths are so big they are often mistaken for birds.

The cabbage moth can often be seen in vegetable gardens.

Female moths can have up to 50 babies at a time.

Baby moths start
life as eggs.

After the eggs
hatch, they turn
into caterpillars.

After seven weeks
they become moths.

Many moths live for only a few days.

Some moths live for up to three months.

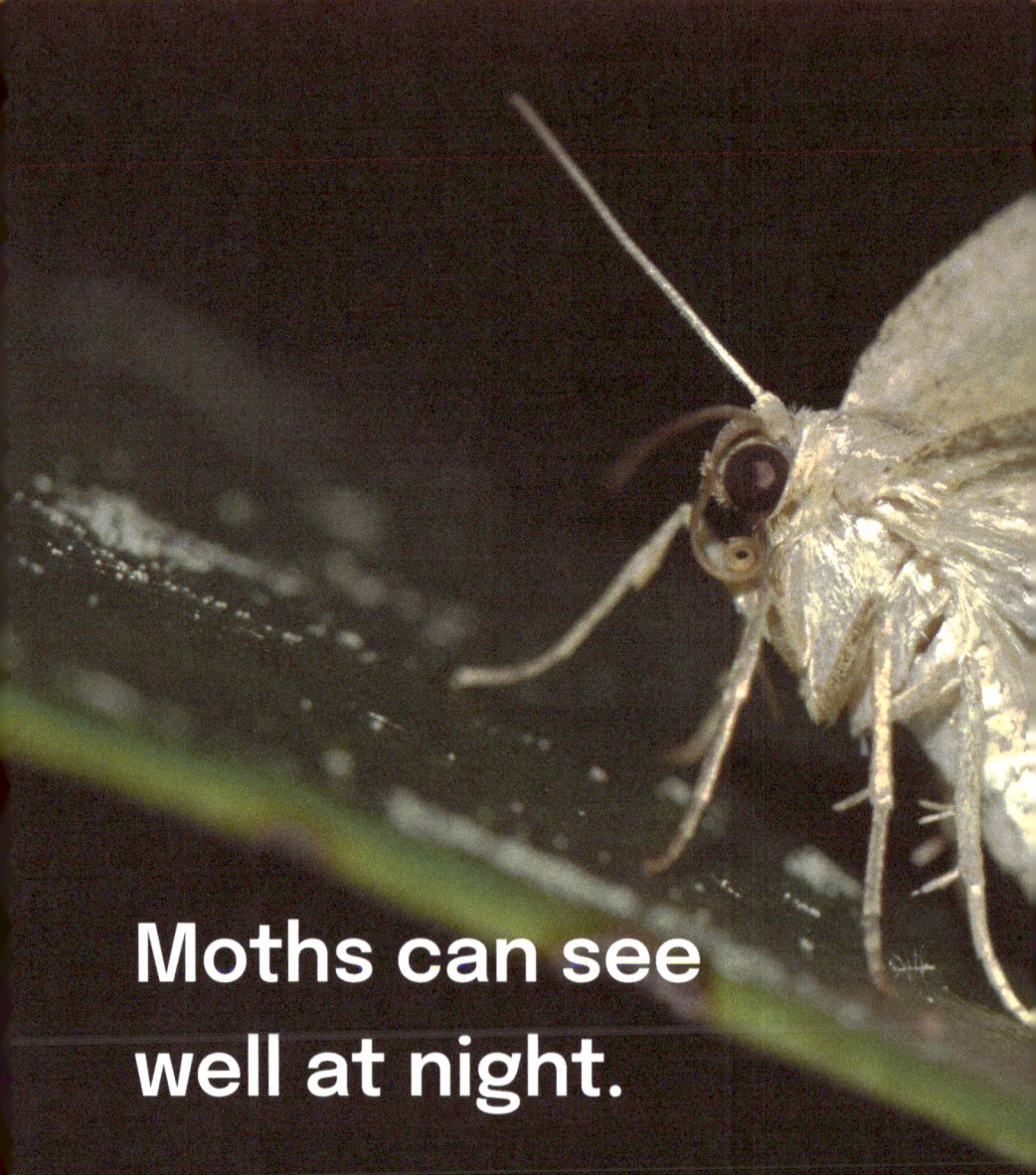

Moths can see
well at night.

Male moths have a great sense of smell.

Moths are very
good at hiding
when in danger.

They pretend to be other insects.

25

Animals and insects eat moths.

In some places
humans eat them!

Explore other books in the Backyard Bugs & Creepy Crawlies series!

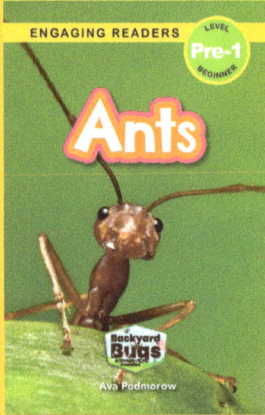

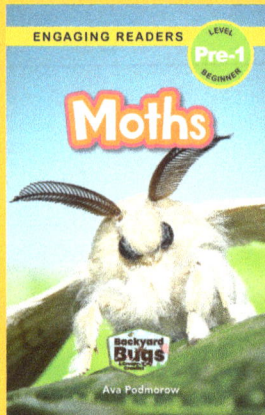

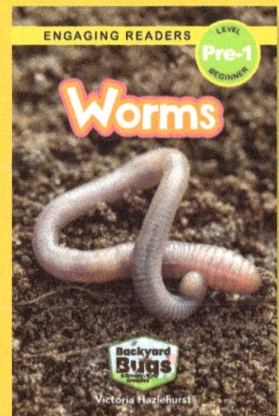

ENGAGING READERS · LEVEL Pre-1 BEGINNER
Ants
Backyard Bugs
Ava Podmorow

ENGAGING READERS · LEVEL Pre-1 BEGINNER
Beetles
Backyard Bugs
Victoria Hazlehurst

ENGAGING READERS · LEVEL Pre-1 BEGINNER
Caterpillars
Backyard Bugs
Ava Podmorow

ENGAGING READERS · LEVEL Pre-1 BEGINNER
Grasshoppers
Backyard Bugs
Ava Podmorow

ENGAGING READERS · LEVEL Pre-1 BEGINNER
Moths
Backyard Bugs
Ava Podmorow

ENGAGING READERS · LEVEL Pre-1 BEGINNER
Snails
Backyard Bugs
Ava Podmorow

ENGAGING READERS · LEVEL Pre-1 BEGINNER
Spiders
Backyard Bugs
Ava Podmorow

ENGAGING READERS · LEVEL Pre-1 BEGINNER
Wasps
Backyard Bugs
Sarah Harvey

ENGAGING READERS · LEVEL Pre-1 BEGINNER
Worms
Backyard Bugs
Victoria Hazlehurst

Visit www.engagebooks.com/readers

Explore books in the Animals In The City series.

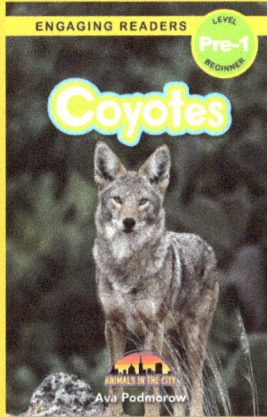

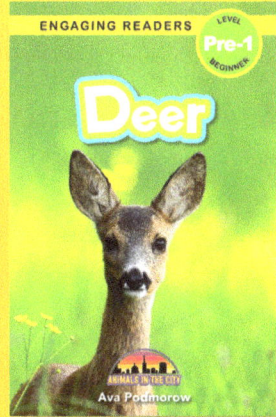

ENGAGING READERS
LEVEL Pre-1 BEGINNER
Cats
ANIMALS IN THE CITY
Ava Podmorow

ENGAGING READERS
LEVEL Pre-1 BEGINNER
Coyotes
ANIMALS IN THE CITY
Ava Podmorow

ENGAGING READERS
LEVEL Pre-1 BEGINNER
Deer
ANIMALS IN THE CITY
Ava Podmorow

ENGAGING READERS
LEVEL Pre-1 BEGINNER
Owls
ANIMALS IN THE CITY
Ava Podmorow

ENGAGING READERS
LEVEL Pre-1 BEGINNER
Pigeons
ANIMALS IN THE CITY
Ava Podmorow

ENGAGING READERS
LEVEL Pre-1 BEGINNER
Rabbits
ANIMALS IN THE CITY
Ava Podmorow

ENGAGING READERS
LEVEL Pre-1 BEGINNER
Raccoons
ANIMALS IN THE CITY
Sarah Harvey

ENGAGING READERS
LEVEL Pre-1 BEGINNER
Rats
ANIMALS IN THE CITY
Ava Podmorow

ENGAGING READERS
LEVEL Pre-1 BEGINNER
Skunks
ANIMALS IN THE CITY
Ava Podmorow

Visit www.engagebooks.com/readers

www.ingramcontent.com/pod-product-compliance
Lightning Source LLC
Chambersburg PA
CBHW051238020426
42331CB00016B/3433